THE BRITISH SOLDIER IN THE 20TH CENTURY

Written and illustrated by

MIKE CHAPPELL

WESSEX MILITARY PUBLISHING

Published in 1989 by
Wessex Military Publishing
1A High Street
Hatherleigh, Devon EX20 3JH
© Copyright 1989 Wessex
Military Publishing

ISBN 1 870498 07 0

Typeset and printed in Great Britain by
Toptown Printers Limited
Vicarage Lawn, Barnstaple, North Devon
England

The author would like to express his thanks for the assistance rendered by the staff of the Welch Regiment Museum during the preparation of this publication. Special thanks are due to the Curator, Bryn Owen, FMA, Lt. R.N. (Retd) for his generous provision of data and photographs. The Welch Regiment Museum is one of the finest the author has visited. Set in the splendid surroundings of Cardiff's Castle, which is itself in the centre of this busy and interesting city, the Museum should not be missed. (The Welch Regiment Museum of the Royal Regiment of Wales (24th/41st Foot), the Black and Barbican Towers, the Castle, Cardiff, CF1 2RB, Wales).

Above: Lieutenant W.T.B. Rhodes, 1st Welsh, in February 1900. Note the gold piping in the crown of his dark blue field service cap (other ranks wore a plain cap), his cap and collar badges, and the "Welsh" titles below his badges of rank. His khaki jacket is in serge, and both braces of his Sam Browne equipment are worn. (All photographs used in the illustration of this publication have been provided by the Welch Regiment Museum and are reproduced by its courtesy.)

Below: A gun of the Maxim machine gun sections, 1st Welsh, at the turn of the century. Still "Redcoats" on home service prior to the introduction of 1902 drab service dress. Note the dark blue field service caps in which other ranks wear the dragon collar badge.

Back cover: The Corps of Drums of the 2nd Bn the Welsh Regiment, Quetta, India, 1906. Note the tropical ceremonial order for men and mascot.

The Welch Regiment

Origins

On the 11th of March 1719 there was raised from among the out-pensioners of the Royal Hospital, Chelsea, a regiment styled "Colonel Edmund Fieldings's Regiment of Invalids". It was employed on guard and anti-smuggling duties until 1787, when it abandoned its invalid character and became a marching regiment of foot. It was by then know as the "41st Regiment of Foot (or Invalids)".

In 1758 the second battalion of the 24th Foot was redesignated the 69th Regiment of Foot, continuing under its new title and precedence to serve the Fleet as Marines.

In January 1760 the Royal Glamorgan Militia was raised, becoming the Royal Glamorgan Light Infantry Militia in 1812.

In 1831 Royal assent was given the 41st to be styled "The 41st Regiment or the Welch Regiment of infantry", thus beginning the Regiment's association with Wales.

In 1881, as a result of the Cardwell Army Reforms, the 41st (The Welch) and the 69th (South Lincolnshire) Regiments were united to form the 1st and 2nd Battalions of the Welsh Regiment. A regimental depot was established in Cardiff and a 3rd (Militia) Battalion (the old Royal Glamorgan) joined the Regiment. Four battalions of rifle volunteers from South Wales were affiliated to the new regiment. These last were redesignated in 1887 to become the 1st, 2nd, 3rd and 4th Volunteer Battalions of the Welsh Regiment, having been the 1st Pembroke Rifle Volunteer Corps, the 1st Glamorgan R.V.C., the 2nd Glamorgan R.V.C, and the 3rd Glamorgan R.V.C., respectively. The last named reverting to its old Rifle Volunteer designation from 1891 to 1908.

This was how the Welsh Regiment was organised as the Twentieth Century dawned. Two regular battalions, the regimental depot in the heart of its recruiting area, a militia battalion and four volunteer battalions. Before the old century died all were to be involved in the conflict that flared up in South Africa.

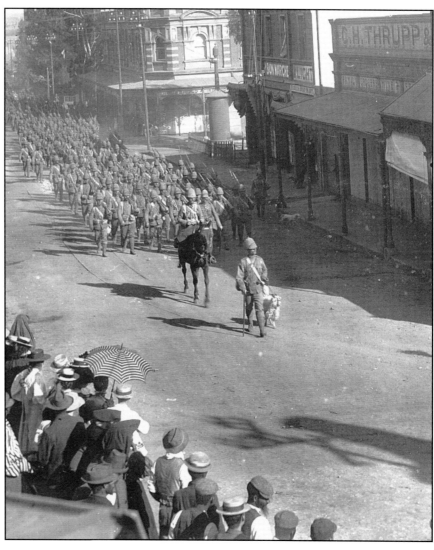

Led by their mascot and with their mounted Commanding Officer at their head, the 1st Welsh enter Pretoria, June 1900. Like other units in Lord Roberts' command they had marched and fought for 300 miles to get to the Boer capital.

The Regiment in the 20th century

During the South African, or Boer War of 1899-1902 the Regiment was represented by the 1st Welsh which had serving with it in succession 3 volunteer service companies drawn from the volunteer battalions of the regiment. Present also was the 3rd (Militia) Battalion which carried out duties on the lines of communication. The 2nd Battalion contributed by sending reinforcement drafts from India to the 1st Battalion.

In 1904 the 1st Welsh left South Africa and returned to the United Kingdom, whilst the 2nd Battalion left Agra in 1906 to take up duties in South Africa. It is of interest to note that the 3rd Volunteer Battalion, up to 1903, was the largest volunteer battalion in the United Kingdom, with the exception of one Scottish volunteer battalion.

1908 saw the implementation of Mr Haldane's Army reorganisation which called for the "standing down" of the old Volunteers and the formation of a Territorial Force. The changes affected the Welsh Regiment as follows:– The 3rd (Militia) Battalion became the 3rd (Special Reserve) Battalion, The Welsh Regiment. A 4th Battalion, The Welsh Regiment (T.F.) was formed around a nucleus of officers and men drawn from the old 1st Volunteer Battalion. A 5th Battalion, The Welsh Regiment (T.F.) was formed around a nucleus drawn from the old 3rd

Types of uniform worn by the 2nd Welsh, Agra, India 1905. The new short rifles and 1903-pattern bandolier equipment had yet to reach this battalion. Buff leather equipment was not pipeclayed (whitened) in India at this time – a health precaution.

Volunteer Battalion. A 6th Battalion, The Welsh Regiment (T.F.) was formed around a nucleus drawn from the old 3rd Glamorgan Rifle Volunteer Corps at Swansea. A 7th (Cyclist) Battalion, The Welsh Regiment (T.F.) was formed around a nucleus of officers and men drawn from the cyclist sections of the old Glamorgan based volunteer battalions.

The 2nd Volunteer Battalion, with the exception of its cyclists was lost to the Regiment as a result of these changes. It provided officers and men for a Territorial Force artillery brigade, a Royal Horse Artillery battery (T.F.), transport and supply columns, A.S.C. (T.F.) and a Welsh field ambulance.

In 1909 the 1st Welsh was ordered to Egypt and there remained until posted to India in 1914. The 2nd Welsh returned to the United Kingdom in 1910 and was stationed for a period at Pembroke Dock.

The outbreak of the Great War in 1914 found the 1st Welsh at Chakrata, India, and the 2nd Welsh at Bordon Camp, Hampshire. The 3rd (S.R.) Battalion was immediately embodied in Cardiff and commenced the important work of training reservists and recruits as reinforcements for the regular battalions. The territorial battalions, then engaged in their annual training, proceeded to their war stations along the South West Wales coast. Before the end of the year the 1st

Welsh was on its way home to England and the 4th and 5th (T.F.) Battalions had joined the Welsh (T.F.) Division concentrating in Northamptonshire. The 2nd Battalion, meanwhile, as part of the B.E.F., was heavily engaged in the fighting in France and Flanders. It was joined by the 6th (T.F.) Battalion which was initially employed on lines of communication.

The demands of war saw second and third line battalions raised for the Territorial Force, and service and reserve battalions for the New Armies. During the course of the war the Welsh Regiment grew to 35 battalions which served as follows:-

The Regular Battalions – 1st Battalion, Western Front. Macedonia (28th Division). 2nd Battalion, Western Front. Army of Occupation (1st Division).

Special Reserve – 3rd Battalion, training and draft finding.

T.F. Battalions – 1/4th Battalion, Gallipoli, Palestine (53rd Division). 2/4th Battalion, home defence and draft finding. 3/4th Battalion (later 4 Res Bn), home defence and draft finding. 1/5th Battalion, Gallipoli, Palestine (53rd Division). 2/5th, home defence and draft finding. 3/5th (later 5 Res Bn), home defence and draft finding. 1/6th Battalion, Western Front, Army of Occupation (28th Division and pioneers, 1st Division). 2/6th Battalion, home defence and draft finding. 3/6th Bat-

talion (later 6 Res Bn), home defence and draft finding. 1/7th Battalion (Cyclists), Scottish and East Coast defence, 2/7 Batallion (Cyclists), East Coast defence, draft finding. 3/7th Battalion (Cyclists), draft finding. 24th (Pembroke and Glamorgan Yeomanry), Palestine and Western Front (74th Division).

New Armies Service and Reserve Battalions – 8th Battalion (Pioneers), Gallipoli, Mesopotamia (13th Division). 9th Battalion, Western Front (19th Division). 10th Battalion (1st Rhondda), Western Front (38th Division). 11th Battalion (Cardiff Pals), Western Front, Macedonia (22nd Division). 12th Battalion (Reserve), draft finding. 13th Battalion (2nd Rhondda), Western Front (38th Division). 14th Battalion (Swansea), Western Front (38th Division). 15th Battalion (Carmarthenshire), Western Front (38th Division). 16th Battalion (Cardiff City), Western Front (38th Division). 17th Battalion (1st Glamorgan Bantams), Western Front (40th Division). 18th Battalion (2nd Glamorgan Bantams), Western Front (40th Divison). 19th Battalion (Glamorgan Pioneers), Western Front (38th Division). 20th Battalion (Reserve), draft finding. 21st Battalion (Reserve), draft finding. 22nd Battalion (Reserve), draft finding, 23rd Battalion (Pioneers), Macedonia (28th Division).

Above: 2nd Welsh preform a guard of Honour for the Prince of Wales (later King Goerge V) Quetta, India 1906. Khaki Wolseley helmets and plain (unpipeclayed) buff equipment contrasts with scarlet tunics and white facings.

Right: Looking more like a cossack than a British soldier; the uniform of Colour Sergeant J.A. Thomas of the cyclist section, 3rd Volunteer Battalion, The Welsh Regiment, in 1902. Note his Torin ("Austrian") cap, cartridges in loops on his chest, star badge for proficiency in sergeants of the Volunteer Force and pouch belt.

Below: The Regimental Police of the 1st Welsh, Gravesend 1906, turned out in service dress and Brodrick caps. Six have "shoulder boards" and two cord shoulder straps. Note the shoulder titles, "Welsh", with the numeral "1" below, G.M.P. (Garrison Military Police) brassards, canes and lack of puttees. All three photographs point up the dress oddities prevalent in a period of great uniform change for the British Army.

The Vickers machine gun began to replace the Maxim from 1912. Here, a detachment of the 3rd (Special Reserve) Battalion, the Welsh Regiment train with a Vickers, Cardiff, November 1914. In the following year all infantry machine gunners were drafted into the Machine Gun Corps.

Young Soldiers Service Battalions – 51st, 52nd and 53rd Battalions, Army of Occupation.

A 25th Service Battalion was raised but was only in existence for twenty days.

By mid 1919 demobilisation had reduced the two regular battalions to cadres, which came together briefly at Pembroke Dock. Both were then brought up to strength, and in August 1919 the 1st Welsh sailed for India, whilst the 2nd Battalion settled down to a period of home service. Meanwhile the Territorial Force battalions had been disembodied and the New Armies battalions demobilised.

A War Office letter dated 27th January, 1920 gave approval for the spelling 'WELCH' to be used in all matters relating to the Regiment, a change confirmed by Army Order 56 of February, 1920. February also saw the reconstitution of the Territorial Force battalions, but under the title Territorial Army, a distinction given to the late Force in recognition of its services during the war.

The 4th, 5th, 6th and 7th Battalions were reformed in March of that year, but by December the 7th Welch had been disbanded and its personnel absorbed by the 6th. The year also saw the dispersal through demobilisation of the Young Soldiers battalions which had been serving with the Army of Occupation in the Rhineland.

Mid June 1920 saw the 2nd Welch ordered to Ireland where it was to serve during the difficult period of the implementation of the Home Rule Act. Meanwhile the 1st Battalion had settled in to a three year period of duty at Ferozepore.

In November 1922 the 1st Welch moved to Peshawar preparatory to marching up to Razmak in Waziristan, North West Frontier, where the Mahsud tribe was openly hostile to road development in their country. In December, the 2nd Battalion, having handed over Richmond Barracks, Dublin, to the Irish Free State Army, moved to Colchester. On the 13th March, 1924, the 1st Welch returned to India and took up duties in Bareilly.

In March, 1927 the 1st Welch moved to Aden and thence back to the United Kingdom to take up duties at New Barracks, Gosport. At about this time the 2nd Welch was ordered to China as part of a special China Defence Force. The battalion arrived in Shanghai on the 3rd September and joined the 14th Infantry Brigade at the Great Western Road Camp. But by the end of 1928 the 2nd Welch moved on to Singapore and Tanglin Barracks. At home an alliance was established between the Regiment and the Ontario Regiment of Canada.

In 1931 the 2nd Welch moved to India and was posted to Roberts Barracks, Rawalpindi. The Battalion

moved up to Landi Kotal Camp in the Khyber Pass in 1934 where it remained until 1936. At home an alliance was established between the 45th Battalion (St George Regiment) Australian Military Forces and the Welch Regiment. The 1st Welch, after service in Gosport and Aldershot, moved to Belfast in November 1935 and was quartered in Victoria Barracks. In India, meanwhile, the 2nd Welch was stationed in Agra.

In November 1938 the 6th Welch, T.A. was converted to a searchlight role and designated 6th Bn, The Welch Regiment (67th S.L. Regt) T.A. By that conversion the battalion was eventually lost to the Welch Regiment, its lineage and traditions today being perpetuated in 104 Regiment, R.A. (V).

In May 1939 the 1st Welch moved from Belfast to Palestine where it was to be heavily involved in internal security duties. At home, the threat of war resulted in a duplication of the Territorial Army, which in respect of the Welch Regiment resulted in the formation of two additional battalions, the 2/4th in Llanelli (shortly thereafter renumbered 15th Welch) and the 2/5th in Swansea. Both battalions started to form in March 1939.

(continued on page 18)

Improving the range and rate of the infantry's mobility represented a considerable problem in the early years of the 20th Century. Experience in the Boer War of 1899-1902 confirmed the importance of mounted infantry in the British Army. Not only horses and ponies were used in this role; the 1st Welsh M.I. detachment utilised camels in Egypt, 1911 *(above, left)*. The uniform equipment and saddlery of the mounted infantry officer are demonstrated by Captain E.L. Wilcox, 1st Welsh, Cairo 1912 *(above, right)*. In the European context, cycles were thought to be the answer. *Below:* the cyclists of the 7th Welsh (T.F.) parade with their steeds in Cardiff, 1911.

1

2

3

4

5

The 1st Welsh arriving in South Africa in 1899 wore Slade-Wallace equipment with the battalion's title painted on the valises. Cap badges were pinned through a shoulder-strap on the right of the helmet (figure top left). An example, in the Regimental Museum (photograph below) indicates that insignia was modified during the course of the war.

The 1st Welsh were photographed in England in 1906 wearing Service Dress, Brodrick caps, and wearing the "Mounted Infantry" equipment shown by the figure at top, centre. Officers adopted the style of Service Dress shown at bottom, left. In the 6th Welsh (T.F.) in 1909 the subalterns sported shoulderstraps woven from cords in the Regimental colours. 6th Welsh officers also wore cap badges on their collars, with the regulation "T" pinned below. Other ranks wore the "General Service" button and cloth titles, but officers wore Regimental-pattern buttons (both are shown in detail, bottom, left).

A full-dress uniform continued to be worn up to 1914, none being more striking than that of the 7th (Cyclist) Bn, the Welsh Regiment, (Territorial Force). The main figure on the plate is that of the Signals Sergeant of the 7th. Note his qualification badges for shooting, signals instructing and 15 years efficient service. His medals are the Queen's South Africa Medal and the Territorial Efficiency Medal. Shoulderstrap detail is shown at bottom, right.

At left, 4, is the badge worn on the pouch at the rear of the pouch-belt by officers and sergeants of the 7th.

On the same photograph at 1 is the Officer's home service helmet plate 1881-1902. A later version is being worn in the photograph at bottom, left, by officers of the 2nd Welsh entraining for strike-breaking duties in Liverpool, 1912. At 5 is the bronzed version of the cap badge worn by officers in Service Dress. At 2 is the cap badge of the Welsh Brigade 1960-69, and at 3 the cap badge of the Royal Regiment of Wales.

COLOUR PLATE B

The length of a "short" Lee-Enfield rifle with bayonet fixed is about 5 feet 1 inch to 5 feet 2 inches. Just about the height of the Great War "Bantams", men between 5 feet and 5 feet 3 inches in height, recruited for service after the initial rush to the Colours. History records that the Bantam experiment was not, in the main, a success – but the tough little ex-miners from South Wales proved to be the exception to the rule, able to withstand the rigours of warfare as well as any. The main figure on this plate depicts a private of the 18th (2nd Glamorgan) Welsh, 40th (Bantam) Division, 1917. The insignia on his jacket indicates Division, Brigade and unit, over two years service and a wound. His equipment is the 1914-pattern.

In the same year the 1st Welsh were serving in Salonika with the 28th Division. They wore a red cloth version of the Prince of Wales' plumes on their slouch hats and the insignia of their Division on their shoulder-straps (top, centre). The "plumes", cut out of the cloth, were used by other battalions (that shown in blue by the 8th) and the full crest was chosen as the sign of the 53rd (Welsh) Division, T.F. Other battalions used pieces of ribbon in the regimental colours, the two configurations used by the 1/6th being illustrated.

At top, right a Second Lieutenant of the 4/5th (amalgamated 1/4th and 1/5th) Welsh, 53rd Division, is depicted in Palestine, 1918. (The uniform is from an example in the Regimental Museum.) From Palestine to the Western Front in this year came the 74th Yeomanry Division, which included the 24th Welsh who wore the badge of the "broken spur" as shown.

At bottom right is depicted a Sergeant of the 16th Welsh (City of Cardiff) in 1919. Note the Dragon patch of the 38th (Welsh) Division, the all-brass wartime economy cap-badge, "Welch" titles (worn only by this battalion) and the Cardiff City arms collar badges. Six battalions of the Regiment served with the 38th Division, wearing the circles and square patches shown on their right sleeves. Shown below in detail is the "slip-on" title worn during the Great War.

The photographs at right show, (top to bottom) a group of N.C.O.s of 2nd Welsh in reserve at Loos, 1916; a group of officers of the same battalion in a trench at Givenchy, 1915, and a group of officers of the 1/5th Welsh in Palestine, 1917.

The power exercised by a Regimental Sergeant Major has alway
ment of R.S.M. still needs a lot of living up to. The Welch Reg
Burns, MM, of the 2nd Welch, 1934. *At right:* R.S.M. Tudor Price
O.R. helmet plate 1902-1914. (3) Officers white metal cap ba
Shoulder-titles. (6) O.R., gilding metal up to 1920. (7) Officer
(10) O.R., G.M., 5th Bn 1908-20. Similar patterns were worn by
38. Similar titles with "5" worn by 5th Bn. (12) O.R., G.M. befor
Full Dress etc 1881-1902. (14) O.R., G.M., Full Dress etc 1881-1
T.F. Bns with 'T' below 1908-14, and badge alone until WWII;
metal by Officers and O.R. 2nd and 3rd V.B. 1887-1908, Full Dr
O.R. of 7th Bn 1912-20 Full Dress and K.D. (19) Officers and C
Pioneer battalions during the Great War. Officers wore similar
of Cardiff were issued to the first 1,000 recruits for the 16th B
only by the survivors of the first 1,000 to volunteer.

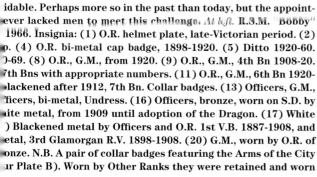

idable. Perhaps more so in the past than today, but the appoint-
ever lacked men to meet this challenge. At left, R.S.M. "Bobby"
1966. Insignia: (1) O.R. helmet plate, late-Victorian period. (2)
p. (4) O.R. bi-metal cap badge, 1898-1920. (5) Ditto 1920-60.
0-69. (8) O.R., G.M., from 1920. (9) O.R., G.M., 4th Bn 1908-20.
7th Bns with appropriate numbers. (11) O.R., G.M., 6th Bn 1920-
lackened after 1912, 7th Bn. Collar badges. (13) Officers, G.M.,
ficers, bi-metal, Undress. (16) Officers, bronze, worn on S.D. by
ite metal, from 1909 until adoption of the Dragon. (17) White
) Blackened metal by Officers and O.R. 1st V.B. 1887-1908, and
etal, 3rd Glamorgan R.V. 1898-1908. (20) G.M., worn by O.R. of
onze. N.B. A pair of collar badges featuring the Arms of the City
ar Plate B). Worn by Other Ranks they were retained and worn

The Welch Regiment experienced soldiering on India's North West Frontier on two occasions between the World Wars. The photograph at top, left shows "Goat Picket", Razmak, garrisoned by a detachment of the 1st Welch in 1924. (Note the wire, "sangar" walling, cleared fields of fire, and the Lewis Gun on the left.) Ten years later the 2nd Welch were on the Frontier. The left-hand figure on the Colour Plate depicts a private of the time dressed for a "ration" fatigue. A strip of ribbon in the Regimental colours (the colours of Wales) is worn as a puggasree flash.

At right, the figure of a Lieutenant of the 1st Welch has been drawn from a description of the dress and equipment worn by a veteran on the morning of the German airborne invasion of Crete, 1941. Note the officer's coloured field service cap, Regimental garter tabs and "desert boots". The detail of this figure's shoulderstrap and garter tabs are shown below. The photograph at bottom, left shows the same battalion five years later in Trieste. At this time the 1st Welch were brigaded with the 3rd Grenadier Guards and the 3rd Welsh Guards in the 6th Armoured Division. They wear the mailed fist sign of their division and white-on-black titles conforming to those worn by the Welsh Guards.

The central figure on the Colour Plate and the centre photograph at left depict the 1/4th Welch in the fighting in North West Europe in the winter of 1944/45. Note the equipment configuration, the wearing of the serge-lined leather jerkin, and the front-line infantryman's preference for the General Service pick and shovel. (The most efficient tools for getting below ground level in a hurry!) A printed title "Welch Regiment" was worn with the Divisional "W" of the 53rd (Welsh) Division, the 3 arm-of-service strips of the 160th Infantry Brigade, and the "Sospan" of the 1/4th Battalion.

The yellow cross of St David was the Divisional sign of the 38th (Welsh) Division of the second World War. (In fact, the second-line Division to the 53rd.) Serving with the 38th were two battalions of the Welch Regiment, the 2/5th and the 15th. The first Welch Regiment title worn on Battledress was the "slip-on" version shown at bottom, left. This was replaced by an embroidered white-on-red title with the legend "The Welch Regiment".

Plate C

WELCH REGIMENT

THE WELCH REGIMENT

COLOUR PLATE D

The central figure of this plate depicts a Company Sergeant Major of the 2nd Welch at Toungoo, Burma 1946. (The dress is identical to that worn by men of the battalion in the photograph on page 22.) The 2nd Welsh were among the first British units to wear the jungle hat, probably the U.S. issue item. A strip of ribbon in the Regimental colours was worn on the left side with the Regimental cap badge at the front. Divisional insignia is worn on the sleeves and badge of rank on a leather wrist strap, worn on the right arm. White webbing and the re-adoption of sergeant's red sashes were an attempt to brighten up jungle-green uniform for ceremonial. The battalion was serving with the 17th "Black Cat" Indian Division, having previously served with the 19th "Dagger" Indian Division, the divisional sign of which is shown in detail at left.

As unusual variety of head dress was worn by the 2nd Welch at this time. As well as the helmet and field service cap, the general service cap was worn with a red patch behind the badge (right). The bush hat was also worn. (The example at right bears the sign of South Burma Command, the old 12th Army, into which the 2nd Welch were transferred from the 17th Division.) Officers of the battalions adopted a green beret, but were ordered to discontinue the practice (right).

The red patch adopted by the 2nd Welch at the end of World War Two continued to be worn on the khaki beret and on the blue beret (left) introduced in the late 1940s.

In the 1950s hosetops with coloured tops began to be issued widely throughout the British Army. Those for the Welch Regiment (bottom right) having red tops. These were worn with the garter flashes previouly in use. Other regimental items of dress worn in the 1950s included the stable belt (left), the brassard (bottom left – badged for a drummer of 1st Welch, Commonwealth Division, Korea 1952), and officer's shoulder "slide" (bottom right – Second Lieutenant).

The photograph at top right shows a group of the 2nd Welch in 1946, posed around a surrendered Japanese machine gun. Note the "American" jungle hats (in which one man has pinned the wartime economy plastic cap badge). Below this is a photograph of Major D.E.B. Salmon, 1st Welch, greeting Captain J Coles of the 45th U.S. Infantry prior to taking over Hill 355, Kowansan, Korea in April 1952.

A draft for the 2/7th (Cyclists) Welsh, T.F., parade at Paddington Station, London, in 1915. Both Welsh Regiment cyclists battalions remained on the defence of the east coast of England throughout the war. Note the unique cycling coats worn in lieu of greatcoats.

September 3rd, 1939 and the outbreak of the second World War found the 1st Welch in Palestine and the 2nd Welch in India. At home the first and second line T.A. battalions mobilised at Pontypridd, Llanelli and Swansea, the first line battalions moving shortly thereafter to Haverfordwest, Pembrokeshire. During the Second World War the various battalions of the Welch Regiment served as follows:- 1st Battalion, Palestine, Libya, Egypt, Crete, Cyrenaica, Sudan, Sicily and Italy (serving with a number of formations). 2nd Battalion, India and Burma (19th Indian Division). 1/4th Battalion, United Kingdom (including a period in Ulster), France and North West Europe (53rd Welsh Division). 1/5th Battalion, same record as 1/4th. 2/5th Battalion, United Kingdom, home defence and draft finding. 15th Battalion, United Kingdom, home defence and draft finding.

Additionally several training battalions were raised for the Regiment during the course of the war, namely the 16th, 17th, 18th, 19th and 70th (Young Soldiers) Battalions. Their function was a mixture of home defence, training and draft finding. Towards the end of the war

they progressively disappeared as their personnel were sent to replace casualties in combat formations.

The 1st Welch suffered particularly during the war, the battle for Crete being a prime example. Having fought a rearguard action, only 8 officers and 161 other ranks escaped to reform the battalion in Egypt. It again suffered heavily in the vicinity of Benghazi in 1942, but reformed in time for the Sicily landings. During the Italian campaign of 1944 it was, as a result of losses, reduced to cadre strength, but was reformed within weeks to take over a sector of the winter line on the River Senio. At Tarvisio, northern Italy on the 8th May, 1945, the 1st Welch received the news that the War in Europe was over. (It remained in Italy until 1947, before returning home after an absence of 8 years.) In Germany the 1/4th and 1/5th Welch celebrated VE Day in Hamburg. Both continued to serve in north west Germany until disbanded in 1946. In Burma, meanwhile, the 2nd Welch, as part of 19 (Dagger) Division of the 14th Army, was still fighting. When VJ Day arrived it was engaged in operations in the Toungoo district.

By the end of 1946 the T.A. and wartime raised battalions had been "stood down", the T.A. battalions being placed in suspended animation. On the 1st March 1947, the 4th Welch at Llanelli and the 5th Welch at Pontypridd were reformed and soon involved in training within their battalion districts.

In October 1947, on returning home, the 1st Welch moved into Woodfarm Camp, Malvern, where before the end of the year it was joined by the 2nd Battalion which had been absent from the United Kingdom for twenty years. At Malvern both battalions found themselves sharing the same barracks for the second time in their history.

In February 1948 the 1st Welch moved to Dering Lines Camp, Brecon, where the battalion was destined to take over the role of Welsh Brigade Training Centre. On the 21st April 1948, the 2nd Battalion was disbanded, so ending a long and distinguished history, today perpetuated in the living Regiment and by the Regimental Museum of 'The Welch' in Cardiff Castle.

(continued on page 24)

The spirit of soldiering in India in the 1930s is captured by the two photographs on this page; both of 2nd Welch. *Above:* the signals platoon pose with their visual signalling equipment. Rawalpindi, 1932. The picture contains a wealth of infomation on the uniform and insignia of the time. "Eight 'undred fightin' Englishmen, the Colonel, and the Band" wrote Kipling. The photograph below shows a company of "fightin" Welshmen of the 2nd Welch with their pack animals being played back to barracks by the full band and drums (who have not accompanied the marching troops all the way). The Colonel is not present, but the essence of route marching "over Injia's coral strand" leaps from the picture after over fifty years. Rawalpindi, 1935.

The Regular Army at home station in peacetime. Aldershot, 1934. *Above:* The Colours, goat major and "Taffy", regimental mascot to the 1st Welch. *Below:* A guard of honour of the same battalion parades for their King and Queen. Two images of an age when spit-and-polish and drill were the foremost means to the end of discipline.

Wartime, and − in the photograph above − "Taffy" and his goat major have moved from the 1st to the 70th (Young Soldiers) Battalion of the Welch Regiment, Hunstanton, 1943. Two years later many of the men trained by the 70th were serving with the 1/5th Welch in the fighting in N.W. Europe. *Below:* A casualty is evacuated, and a Wireless Set No.18 is seen being operated. Note the use of captured enemy clothing and weapons. (In this case German Army grey/white reversible winter smocks, and an Italian Beretta M38A 9mm sub machine gun. The 1/5th Welch served with the famous 53rd (Welsh) Division.

When the Second World War ended the 2nd Welch were in Toungoo, Burma. They were still there in 1946 when the first two photographs on this page were taken. That above shows the provost section, under Sergeant Newbold, MM. They wear a mixture of tailor-made and issue jungle green uniform, and wear a red patch behind the badges in their G.S. caps. At left, the battalion parade for a G.O.C.s inspection. Their dress is depicted in Colour Plate D. The C.O. of 2 Welch and the officer behind him both wear the short-lived green beret adopted by officers of the battalion.

The photograph below depicts a rifle section of the 1st Welch enjoying (?) a sing-song in Korea, 1952. Sitting well in the background is the section commander, Corporal Eric "Taff" McCue – a long-time friend of the author in later years.

Above: **Benghazi, 1959. The 1st Welch quarter guard turns out and pays compliments to a visiting general officer. Note the scarlet-topped hosetops, also the garter tabs.** *Right:* **A rifleman of 1st Welch on exercise in 1968. Note the regimental colours on his jungle hat and the patch of Land Forces, Hong Kong on his sleeve.** *Below:* **Berlin, 1963. Drummers demonstrate some of the orders of dress worn by the 1st Welch at the time.**

The 1st Welch reformed as an active infantry battalion in 1950 and moved to Colchester, where in 1951 it received orders to join the Commonwealth Division in Korea. The battalion arrived at Pusan in November where curious locals were somewhat bemused to see the newly arrived unit disembark, led by a goat. Within 72 hours of their arrival, the 1st Welch, as part of the 29th British Infantry Brigade, took over a reserve sector from the Glosters. Later, moving into forward positions near Yodong, it endured four bitter winter months, confined mainly to patrol activity. Some of these forays resulted in sharp and fiercely contested fire fights. In addition to frost, the battalion experienced bombardment and flood, fortunately with relatively light casualties. In November 1952 the 1st Welch embarked for Hong Kong, where it remained until its return to the U.K. in 1954.

After a short spell at home the 1st Welch moved to B.A.O.R. (Luneburg) in 1956; to Cyprus for anti-terrorist operations in 1957; to Benghazi in 1959, and back to the U.K. for a short spell of home service in 1960. At home a new 6th Battalion, T.A., came into existence by the conversion of 16th (Welsh) Bn, The Parachute Regiment (which had been formed in March 1947).

In 1958 a Welsh Brigade depot responsible for training recruits for all three Welsh infantry regiments was established at Crickhowell, Breconshire. The three regiments, The Royal Welch Fusiliers, the South Wales Borderers and The Welch then adopted a common cap badge, a particularly upright design of the plumes, coronet and motto of the Prince of Wales. The change saw the closure of the old regimental depots.

In 1961 the 1st Welch moved to Berlin where it was to serve until 1963. Then followed a period of service as demonstration battalion at the School of Infantry prior to moving to Hong Kong for garrison duty in 1966.

Reductions and reorganisation in the Army in the late 1960s required the Welsh Brigade to lose one battalion. In consequence, it was decided to amalgamate the 1st South Wales Borderers and 1st Welch. A "Prince of Wales' Division" was formed with headquarters at Lichfield. The "Division" was to administer the regiments of the former Welsh, Wessex and Mercian Brigades and train their recruits. More drastic was the reform of the Territorial Army, savagely reduced and renamed the Territorial and Army Volunteer Reserve. In Wales existing units were swept away and replaced with a "category T.A.V.R. II" unit styled "The Welsh Volunteers", with its HQ in Cardiff, an 'A' Company represented the Royal Welch Fusiliers, a 'B' Company the South Wales Borderers and a 'C' Company, The Welch. The Welch Regiment contribution was made up from elements of the old 5th and 6th T.A. Battalions. Other elements reformed as T.A.V.R. Category III units, styled 'Territorials', with the role of home and civil defence. Thus came into fairly short-lived existence the 4th (T) and 5/6th (T) Battalions, The Welch Regiment, still based upon the old T.A. battalion districts.

The 1st Welch returned to the United Kingdom in 1968 and during the year carried out public duties in London. On the 14th March, 1969 The Welch celebrated its 250th Anniversary with a parade at the Royal Hospital, Chelsea. In this year also the 4th (T) and 5/6th (T) Battalions were reduced to cadre strength. On the 11th June 1969, the Royal Regiment of Wales was formed by the amalgamation of the 1st South Wales Borderers and the 1st Welch at a ceremony in the grounds of Cardiff Castle, at which Colours were presented to the new regiment by The Prince of Wales. At the end of the parade, His Royal Highness, Colonel-in-Chief of the Regiment, received on its behalf, the Freedom of the City of Cardiff.

Customs and Traditions

The Motto
'Gwell Angau na Chywilydd' (Better Death than Dishonour)
Regimental Music
Quick March – Ap Shenkin
                    (strictly Siencyn')
Slow March – Men of Harlech

'The Lincolnshire Poacher' was also popular with the 2nd Battalion, it having been the quick march of the 69th (South Lincolnshire) Regiment, 'Jenny Jones' and 'The Rising of the Lark' were also frequently played, particularly on New Year's Eve, and when in camp at reveille.

The Goat Mascot
There can be little doubt that this custom originated during the Crimean War when the 41st (The Welch) Regiment was involved in the siege of Sevastopol. A goat of Russian origin was adopted by the Regiment at that time and appears with a group of officers in a photograph taken in 1856 shortly before the Regiment's departure from the Crimea.

The custom was, over the years, adopted by all battalions of the Regiment. On Parade, the goat wore a ceremonial coat of scarlet cloth embroidered with Regimental distinctions and edged in the colour of the Regimental facings. Between the horns was carried a distinctive head plate and the horns were adorned with silver horn tips.

Regimental Days
Saint David's Day, March 1st, took precedence over all other special days observed by The Welch Regiment and was celebrated by all battalions of the Regiment. It marked the birth of St David, patron saint of Wales, and gave opportunity in addition to certain special ceremonies for other ranks of the Regiment to view at close quarters the Colours and displays of silver. By the 1920s it had become customary for a distinguished personage or the commanding officer of each battalion to present each officer and man with a leek (the national emblem) to wear in his cap for the day.

The 2nd Battalion also observed the anniversary of the Battle of St Vincent (14th February and Waterloo (18th June) whenever possible. After World War 1, Gheluveldt Day (31st October) was similarly marked.